W9-BPM-988

George Bush

George Bush

Business Executive and U.S. President

ROBERT GREEN

Ferguson Publishing Company
Chicago, Illinois

Photographs ©: AP/Wideworld: 17, 19, 20–21, 25, 33, 37, 46, 49, 51, 62, 64–65, 71, 76–77, 80, 93, 95, 96–97, 98; Corbis: 44, 57; Liaison: 10, 14, 30, 34, 40-41, 78, 81, 85, 86, 90–91.

An Editorial Directions Book

Library of Congress Cataloging-in-Publication Data

Green, Robert, 1969–
    George Bush : business executive and U.S. president / by Robert Green.
    p. cm. — (Ferguson's career biographies)
    Includes bibliographical references (p.) and index.
    ISBN 0-89434-339-4
    1.Bush, George, 1924– —Juvenile literature. 2. Presidents—United States—Biography—Juvenile literature. 3. Businessmen—Texas—Biography—Juvenile literature. 4. Bomber pilots—United States—Biography—Juvenile literature. [1. Bush, George, 1924– 2. Presidents.] I. Title. II. Series.

E882 .G76 2000
973.928'092—dc21
[B]   00-037650

Copyright © 2000 by Ferguson Publishing Company
Published and distributed by
Ferguson Publishing Company
200 West Jackson Boulevard, Suite 700
Chicago, Illinois 60606
www.fergpubco.com

Printed in the United States of America
X-8

CONTENTS

George Bush

FLIGHT OF THE AVENGER

T 7:15 A.M. ON SEPTEMBER 2, 1944, the plane flown by Ensign George Herbert Walker Bush, future president of the United States, was catapulted from the flight deck of the USS *San Jacinto*. His target was the craggy island of Chichi Jima, a communications post for the Japanese navy.

Bush had enlisted in the U.S. Navy after hearing of Japan's surprise attack on the U.S. Pacific fleet at Pearl Harbor, Hawaii, on December 7, 1941. Bush was horrified by the thought of so many neutral American sailors

In uniform. George Herbert Walker Bush served as a pilot in the U.S. Navy during World War II.

perishing with their hulking battleships burned and sunk in the waters of Pearl Harbor. The United States had been drawn into World War II. At the age of eighteen—and against the wishes of his parents— Bush joined the navy.

After recovering from the attack at Pearl Harbor, the U.S. Navy waged ferocious battles to drive the Japanese off the islands dotting the Pacific Ocean. By 1944, the navy was closing in on the Japanese home islands.

Chichi Jima lay only 600 miles (965 kilometers) from Japan itself. Its defense was vital to the Japanese because it was home to a communications center that relayed commands to the Japanese navy. Task Force 58, a U.S. squadron of torpedo bombers, was assigned to destroy Chichi Jima. Accompanied by twenty-six F6F Hellcat fighters to protect the bombers, the squadron pilots, including Bush, took off that September morning.

Bush flew a TBM Avenger torpedo bomber, officially named the *Tare Three*. He called it "Barbara," after the girl he planned to marry as soon as he got home. Bush piloted the stocky, barrel-shaped plane while two crew members manned the machine guns and navigated. The Avenger's large bomb bay had earned it the nickname Pregnant Turkey. Bush described it as looking like "some aberrant fowl."

The V-shaped formation of U.S. bombers reached Chichi Jima about an hour after leaving the *San Jacinto*. As the U.S. planes pounded the island, the skies filled with black smoke and whizzing rounds of ammunition from Japanese antiaircraft guns. "The Japanese were ready and waiting," Bush wrote. As he began his bombing run on the radio towers of Chichi Jima, the plane howled under the pressure.

"Suddenly, there was a jolt, as if a massive fist had crunched into the belly of the plane," he remembered. "Smoke poured out of the cockpit, and I could see flames ripping across the crease of the wing, edging toward the fuel tanks." The Japanese had hit his plane.

Bush held his course and released his bombs over the target. Once the bombs were away, he headed out to sea. His engines sputtered, and smoke poured through the plane. "Hit the silk!" he yelled, ordering his crew to bail out. After pushing back the canopy of the Avenger, the skinny 6-foot, 2-inch (188-centimeter) pilot climbed onto the wing and prepared to jump. But Bush pulled the rip cord of his parachute too soon, and the wind caught his chute and tore him off the wing. As he fell backward, his head struck the plane's tail.

With blood dripping from his forehead, the young pilot fell into one of the deepest parts of the Pacific—the Bonin Trench. Once in the water, Bush was able to unbuckle his chute and swim toward an inflatable life raft that had fallen with him.

The Japanese had seen Bush drop into the sea and sent an armed ship to pick him up. Bush paddled farther out to sea in the tiny raft. An F6F Hellcat circled overhead to protect him. Fortunately, an American submarine, the USS *Finback*, was also nearby, and it now zeroed in on the downed pilot. Armed with only a dagger and a .38 caliber revolver, Bush knew he would be no match for the approaching Japanese!

Bush waited for three hours while both the *Finback* and the Japanese ship raced toward him. He was exhausted, his head was bleeding, and he vomited repeatedly over the side of the raft. As the Japanese ship closed in, the Hellcat swooped down and strafed its decks with machine-gun fire, buying Bush more time.

At 11:58 A.M., the *Finback* finally reached Bush. "You can imagine," Bush wrote to his parents," how

Bush's plane was shot down by the Japanese, but the future president was rescued by an American submarine, the USS Finnback.

happy I was when I saw this submarine. . . . They pulled me out of the raft and took me below where they fixed me up in grand style."

Bush was awarded the Distinguished Flying Cross for his adventure. His crewmates were not so lucky, however. American pilots had seen another flier leaving the plane with a parachute, but it never opened. The third crew member almost certainly died in the crash of the Avenger.

Later, Bush found out just how gruesome his fate might have been had the *Finback* not reached him in time. "Right after the war," he wrote, "the Japanese commander in charge of Chichi Jima was tried and executed for eating the livers of captured American pilots. I like to tease Barbara [the girl he married a few months later] that I almost ended up becoming an hors d'oeuvre." By joining the navy, George Bush displayed qualities cherished by his family—independence, leadership, and above all, public service.

A Connecticut Yankee

George Herbert Walker Bush was born on June 12, 1924, in Milton, Massachusetts. His father, Prescott Bush, had moved there from the Midwest to work for the Stedman Company. The Stedman Company made rubber floor tiling, so Prescott Bush listed his occupation on George's birth certificate as "rubber manufacturer."

While Prescott Bush spent his days at the office, his wife, Dorothy, made a home for George and his older brother, Prescott Jr. They lived in a large Victorian house in leafy, suburban Milton. George's mother grew up in a privileged family at a time when it was unfashionable to educate women in anything other than social etiquette. Nevertheless, Dorothy—or Dotty as she was called—was the moral backbone of the family, guarding her children against the snobbishness that grew along with Prescott's increasing wealth.

Before his first birthday, George's family moved to Greenwich, Connecticut. Greenwich was a wealthy community, made up mostly of successful businessmen from New York City. Every day, his father rode the train to work in New York City.

George lived as safe and peaceful a childhood as any boy in America. In Greenwich, his mother Dorothy had three more children: Nancy, Jonathan, and William (Bucky). But George and Prescott Jr., who was two years older, were closest. When Prescott Jr. entered Greenwich Country Day School,

Five-year-old George with his sister, Nancy. The Bush children grew up in the wealthy community of Greenwich, Connecticut.

George was so depressed that his parents let him go to school a year early to be with his brother. Though he was much smaller than Prescott Jr., George earned the respect of the older boys by excelling at sports. He had, said Prescott Jr., "a good pair of eyes, good hands, natural reactions, and he caught and hit the ball well. He's always been quick and bright."

The Country Day School taught George the classic subjects, including Latin, which would help him get into other top schools. With a cook, a maid, and a chauffeur, the Bush family was well on its way to a place in the social register of Greenwich. But George's mother did not allow snobbery to sprout roots in her children. "She didn't care about all that," recalled his sister Nancy. "That was an unimportant thing. She wouldn't be in the social register."

Once, when George complained that his tennis game was off, his mother tartly reminded him, "You don't have a game." Later George said his mother taught him about "dealing with life in an old-fashioned way of bringing up family—generous measures of both love and discipline."

In the summers, the Bush family moved to Kennebunkport, Maine, to a ten-bedroom summerhouse bought by George's grandfather, George Herbert

George with his older brother, Prescott Jr. The two boys were inseparable throughout their childhood.

Walker. George was not only named after his grandfather, but inherited his nickname—Pop. To avoid confusion, George was often called Little Pop, or Poppy, and the name stuck well into his adulthood.

The Bush family spent summers at this house in Kennebunkport, Maine. The property is comprised of 10 acres bordering the Atlantic Ocean.

The Kennebunkport summer home was situated on a 10-acre (4-hectare) point that jutted into the Atlantic Ocean. For Poppy, the Kennebunkport house was as much his home as Greenwich. Year after year, he swam in the chilly ocean and prayed during services in Kennebunkport's Episcopal Church. "There was a seasonal quality to our lives," his sister Nancy later said. "Our childhood was like a beautiful dream."

When George graduated from the Greenwich Country Day School, he was admitted to Phillips Academy at Andover, Massachusetts. Andover is a prestigious boarding school concerned with shaping the character and intellect of its students.

The school's motto, *Non Sibi*, meaning "Not for Self," mirrored George's family belief in public service. The school's rigid discipline in academics and emphasis on fair play and leadership on the playing field was designed to shape future leaders of the nation.

Bush entered Andover in 1937, when the Democratic president, Franklin Delano Roosevelt, was attempting to remedy the effects of the Great Depression, a worldwide slump in business that struck after the stock market crash of 1929. The Great Depression wiped out the savings of millions of middle-class people and forced many out of work. To combat the depression, Roosevelt used government money to fund projects designed to put Americans back to work.

President Roosevelt's projects were very different from those of other presidents. Many Republicans thought Roosevelt's New Deal was dangerous, believing that he was leading the country toward socialism, a system under which the federal government would own industry and employ citizens directly.

The students at Andover, who were just learning about American politics, repeated the criticism they overheard at home that Roosevelt, a rich man, was a traitor to his class.

At Andover, Bush's athletic ability made him captain of both the baseball and soccer teams. "He just stood out," recalled Frank DiClemente, one of his coaches. "During recess, when the kids had free time, there was this kid [Bush]—just the way he impressed me, all arms and legs, having a helluva good time, laughing. Everybody liked the kid."

Though Bush didn't get the best grades, his flair for leadership was unquestioned. This quality would soon be called upon outside of school.

War erupted in Europe in 1939, when German leader Adolf Hitler invaded Poland. As the Germans marched through the rest of Europe, their allies, the Japanese, were conquering Asia and the Pacific Islands. Most Americans believed that they could stay out of the war, while President Roosevelt repeatedly resisted requests from the British to declare war on Germany.

The matter was finally decided—not by Roosevelt, or the Germans, or the British, but by the Japanese. On December 7, 1941, Japan bombed Pearl Harbor, Hawaii. It was a great victory for Japan, because it destroyed much of the U.S. Navy.

News of a Japanese attack on American soil changed America's mind about declaring war. George Bush reacted in disbelief. "I'll never forget it," he recalled. "I was walking across the campus there near the chapel—it was Sunday—with a friend of mine. And somebody yelled across at us, and it just made a profound impact at that very moment."

Bush jumped at the chance to get out and do something. It was not only his duty, he thought, but an opportunity to make a difference in the world. On his eighteenth birthday—June 12, 1942—Bush enlisted in the U.S. Navy.

After a ten-month flight course, George Bush was awarded his gold wings, making him the youngest commissioned pilot in the U.S. Navy at the time. Bush entered the war with "Christian innocence," a cousin later said. He felt he was ful-filling a noble duty, and he objected to the way his trainers portrayed the Japanese. "It is really sick-ening," Bush wrote to his parents about the military leaflets. "Stuff like 'Kill the Japs—hate—murder' . . . All the well-educated fellows know what they are fighting for—why they are here and don't need to be 'brainwashed' into anything."

George with his brother Bucky in 1942. That year, George turned eighteen and immediately enlisted in the U.S. Navy.

Bush served three years in the navy, flew fifty-eight combat missions, and won the Distinguished Flying Cross. He had also seen his best friends die in the fiery wreck of the downed Avenger over

Chichi Jima. "As I look back," Bush wrote, "I realize how protected my life had been until I joined the Navy. . . . As a result, my vision of the world was narrow, and I was a little judgmental at age eighteen. Like most young people, my horizon needed expanding."

As the Allies prepared for the final invasion of the Japanese home islands, President Harry Truman ordered the use of the atomic bomb on Japan. On the morning of August 6, 1945, the city of Hiroshima disappeared in a single flash of blinding radioactive light. Never in history had an attack been so swift and so devastating—a single bomb destroyed an entire city. Three days later, the port city of Nagasaki, famous for its large Christian population and the Mitsubishi shipyard that built Japan's navy, was destroyed by a second bomb. Emperor Hirohito announced the surrender of Japan less than a week later. World War II was over.

"Whenever I hear anyone criticize President Truman's decision to drop the atomic bomb on Hiroshima and Nagasaki," Bush wrote, "I wonder whether the critic remembers those days and has really considered the alternative: millions of fighting men killed on both sides, possibly tens of millions of

Japanese civilians. Harry Truman's decision wasn't just courageous—it was farsighted. He spared the world and the Japanese people an unimaginable holocaust."

OILMAN

USH RETURNED TO CIVILIAN LIFE in 1945 determined to make up for lost time. For George Bush, the peace meant throwing himself headlong into establishing a family and a career.

Just before Bush shipped out for the Pacific, he met sixteen-year-old Barbara Pierce at a dance at the Round Hill Country Club in Greenwich. The lanky, uncertain dancer got a friend to introduce him to Barbara. For the rest of the night the couple sat down while others danced to the songs of Glenn Miller. Instead, the couple lost themselves in conversation.

Wedding day. George Bush and Barbara Pierce were married on January 6, 1945, in Rye, New York.

"It was a storybook meeting," Bush wrote, "though most couples that got serious about each other in those days could say the same about the first time they met. Young people in the late 1930s and early 1940s were living with what modern psychologists call heightened awareness, on the edge. It was a time of uncertainty, when every evening brought dramatic radio newscasts—Edward R. Murrow from London, William L. Shirer from Berlin—reporting a war we knew was headed our way."

When he entered the U.S. Navy, Bush wrote Barbara a flurry of letters. The relationship progressed quickly. On leave after flight training, Barbara joined the Bush family at Kennebunkport for their summer holiday, and the two became secretly engaged. "Secret," wrote Bush, "to the extent that the German and Japanese high commands weren't aware of it." On January 6, 1945, the two were married at the First Presbyterian Church in Barbara's hometown of Rye, New York.

On the G.I. Bill

Bush threw himself into peacetime activities with great vigor. The two set up home in New Haven, Connecticut, and George Bush enrolled at Yale University, where both his father and grandfather had gone to school.

Bush attended Yale on the G.I. Bill, which not only paid his tuition but gave him academic credit for his military service. He chose economics as his major, and his course load was heavy.

Bush was still serious about athletics. He made the varsity baseball team in his first year and was captain by his senior year.

His classmates elected him captain for his leadership and likability, even though others on the team were better players. Once again, Bush had been chosen by his peers to lead. "He was one of those fellows," wrote classmate John Chafee, later a U.S. senator from Rhode Island, "who was sort of a golden boy: Everything he did, he did well. . . . My first impression was that he was—and I don't mean this in a derogatory fashion—in the inner set, the movers and shakers, the establishment. I don't mean he put on airs or anything but . . . just everybody knew him." This popular impression led Bush to be inducted into the Skull and Bones Club, the most secret Yale student club.

Even though he was popular, Bush spent little of his free time with his classmates. Instead, he would

While at Yale, Bush played on the university baseball team and was captain his senior year.

go home to see Barbara and his new son, George W. Bush. Later, Bush remembered those peaceful days fondly. "We were still young," he wrote, "life lay ahead of us, and the world was at peace. It was the best of times."

Bush graduated from Yale in 2 1/2 years. He was awarded a prize for Economics and the prestigious Phi Beta Kappa key, a mark of academic success. Now it was time to find a career.

Barbara Bush with her first son, George W. Bush. He was born in July 1946 and was later joined by five other children.

Viva Zapata!

Bush knew he did not want to follow his father into the world of investment banking. When a family friend named Neil Mallon suggested that Bush go to Texas to work in the booming oil business, the idea caught his imagination. Mallon offered Bush a job as an equipment clerk. "There's not much salary," Mallon said, "but if you want to learn the oil business, it's a start."

Bush accepted. He knew that Texas was still a place of rugged individualism, where men grappled with the earth to draw out its precious resources. Giant oil-drilling rigs had sprouted up all over the landscape. Oil production was vital to the industry of the United States, and many people made their fortunes in the oil fields of Texas.

Bush packed his belongings into his 1947 Studebaker—a graduation gift from his parents—and drove to Odessa, Texas. He rented an inexpensive house and set up home for Barbara and his son George. "We had one bedroom, a small kitchen, and a shared bathroom," Bush recalled. "An old water-drip window unit that cranked up like a west Texas dust storm drew cool air into the bedroom on hot summer nights."

Texas was in the middle of an oil boom similar to the Gold Rush of the 1800s, when thousands of men went to mine the western United States for gold.

The promise of oil wealth prompted Bush to leave his job in 1951 and enter a partnership with his friend and neighbor John Overbey. Overbey had been buying and selling oil rights and knew the business inside and out. Bush was good at raising money and was a natural salesman.

The Bush-Overbey Oil Development Company was successful because Bush could bring in investors from the Northeast and because Overbey was a good oil prospector. As the company bought up mineral rights and drilled under the parched earth, it struck oil again and again.

Two brothers, Hugh and William Liedtke, noticed Bush and Overbey's success. The brothers had their own successes in the oil business and decided to expand through a partnership with Bush and Overbey. After they hammered out the terms of a new oil company, they all went to see a Marlon Brando film in downtown Midland. The film, *Viva Zapata!*, was based on the life of Mexican revolutionary Emiliano Zapata.

The new partners, caught up in the thrill of launching a new enterprise, named their company

Bush as president of Zapata Off-Shore. This business was very successful and allowed him to meet all kinds of people.

Zapata Petroleum Corporation. Bush was vice president of the corporation, and Hugh Liedtke, whom one writer had called "the genius of west Texas oil," was president.

Hugh Liedtke had a knack for finding oil. In one field alone, 130 wells spewed forth the black gold. Soon, the Liedtke brothers focused on land-based wells, while Bush went to the Gulf of Mexico and helped start off-shore drilling under the new name Zapata Off-Shore. Off-shore drilling was still a great risk. "But we hadn't named our company Zapata," Bush wrote, "in order to be gun-shy about going into revolutionary, high-risk ventures." And Bush's new off-shore drilling rig, named the *Scorpion*, was soon tapping oil from beneath the Gulf of Mexico.

The success of Zapata Petroleum and Zapata Off-Shore made Bush a wealthy man. The oil industry also allowed him to rub shoulders with all types of people. "The oil field doesn't get credit for the fiber of its people," he wrote. "In those days, most of the oil-field workers didn't have much education. They came from an entirely different background than I did. But the way they devoted their lives to their work, their fierce loyalty, competitiveness, and spirit, were an inspiration."

Along the way, George Bush had also suffered one of the greatest losses of his life. In 1949, Barbara had given birth to Robin, the Bush's first daughter. George was delighted to have a daughter. "She'd fight and cry and play and make her way just like the rest," he recalled. "But there was about her a certain softness. . . . Her peace made me feel strong, and so very important." But in 1953, Bush got a call from a Midland doctor. Barbara had taken Robin to the doctor's office because the child had been listless, but neither of them knew how sick she really was. She had developed advanced leukemia and had only a short time to live. These were dark days, as Bush said later, the darkest in his life. "Barbara and I sustained each other; but in the end, it was our faith that truly sustained us, as gradually but surely, Robin slipped away." After three years and ten months of life, Robin died.

Bush could not grasp the injustice that had visited his family. But he decided that there was nothing to do but go on, and he turned back to his family. The same year as Robin's death, 1953, his second son, John, was born. Over the next five years, while Bush worked at Zapata, he and Barbara had three more children: Neil, Marvin, and, in 1959, another

In 1995, George and Barbara Bush marked their fiftieth year of marriage. Through both joys and sorrows, the family has always remained close.

daughter, Dorothy. "You can imagine," he wrote to fellow employees at Zapata, "how thrilled we are to have a baby girl . . . the boys all gathered around and looked over the new baby with great concern. She looks just like all the others."

PUBLIC SERVANT

N 1952, GEORGE'S FATHER, Prescott Bush, was elected to the U.S. Senate, representing the state of Connecticut. With his father in the senate, George Bush, growing restless with the oil business, weighed his chances for winning for elected office. "Politics is always in the Texas air," Bush wrote, "and beginning in the late 1950s, I began to talk to close friends about my growing interest in public service." But in those days, Texans favored Democrats, and Bush was a Republican. "The advice [my friends] gave me," Bush said, "was that if I was serious about running for office, the sensible thing to do was switch parties."

George's parents campaigning in 1956. Prescott Bush served his home state of Connecticut in the U.S. Senate.

But Bush sensed that Texas politics were changing. The state was prospering, and many Texans no longer believed that the Democratic Party represented their interests. "The Democrats," wrote Bush, "had grown fat and complacent. I felt they'd lost touch with the people."

As a result, Bush rejected the advice to switch parties. "Philosophically I was a Republican," he wrote, "and the idea of a party switch didn't sit well with me." Bush announced his bid for a U.S. Senate seat in the election of 1964.

Bush ran against Democrat Ralph Yarborough. Yarborough, the incumbent, was well known in Texas politics. Even though Yarborough was a fierce opponent of President Lyndon Johnson, Johnson supported Yarborough, and Bush was defeated.

Congressman George Bush

One of the most biting criticisms that Bush had suffered during the Senate campaign was being called a carpetbagger—a candidate who runs for office outside his home area. After sixteen years in Texas, Bush considered himself a Texan and was determined to represent the state in some capacity.

A young politician. George Bush ran for the U.S. Senate in 1964, but he was defeated by his Democratic opponent.

The Senate's 100 members—2 from every state—have more power than congressmen, who are elected for only two-year terms. In 1966, Bush set his sights a little lower, announcing that he would run for Congress. "In Midland I was bitten by the bug that led me into the oil business," he wrote. "Now I'd been bitten by another bug."

Bush faced a conservative Democrat in the 1966 election. Because both candidates shared many of the same positions, Bush launched a public-relations campaign to portray himself as a man who could get things done in Washington. "Elect George Bush to Congress and watch the action," read his campaign posters. It worked, and Bush became the first Republican ever to represent Houston.

Congressman George Bush now had the chance to represent the state that had given him his start in the world. He quickly won a reputation as a hardworking straight shooter. He enjoyed the trust of his colleagues, who respected his ability to compromise and be fair. Bush was a moderate conservative, which helped him work with the Democrats in the House of Representatives.

Bush won a seat on the House Ways and Means Committee, which is considered by many to be the most powerful committee in Congress. The Ways and Means Committee controls the nation's budget, and deals with taxation and the funding of new programs.

Bush worked hard to learn the details of government spending and the politics of passing a bill. His voting record matched his conservative views. For example, he spoke against the public accommodations provision of the 1964 Civil Rights Act, arguing that the states could deal with local issues better than the federal government could.

He also supported the war in Vietnam. The United States went to war because it was afraid of a Communist victory. In Vietnam, the Soviet Union backed North Vietnam and the United States backed South Vietnam. In 1968, Republican Richard Nixon replaced Democrat Lyndon Johnson as president, after pledging to end U.S. involvement in Vietnam.

Although Bush supported Nixon's policies, he was still more liberal than many Texans. Bush voted his conscience, supporting open-housing legislation that increased the rights of minority groups to choose where they lived—an idea that was unpopular in Texas. He also upset conservative Republicans by supporting birth-control programs.

New Man at the United Nations

Bush was elected to a second term in 1968, and in 1970, he ran again for the Senate. Again, he lost to a conservative Democrat. President Nixon, who had urged him to try to capture the Senate seat for the Republicans, rewarded Bush by appointing him Permanent Representative to the United Nations (UN).

Another defeat. In 1970, Bush again lost a bid for the U.S. Senate, this time to Houston native Lloyd Bentsen.

Bush's assignment to the UN came at an important time for U.S. foreign policy. American soldiers were still fighting in Vietnam; the threat of nuclear war still loomed; and Communist China was outraged that the United States recognized the government in exile on the island of Taiwan as the legitimate rulers of China.

Bush feared that he would be caught off guard at meetings with UN delegates from other countries, many of whom had years of experience in international matters. He plowed through books and newspapers trying to get up to speed. "In no time at all," wrote one of his aides, "he won their confidence. And you talk to almost anybody in the secretariat [the permanent UN personnel] and they will tell you that he turned out to be an outstandingly effective American representative."

Bush moved his family to New York City, where they occupied a nine-room apartment at the Waldorf Towers, not far from the UN headquarters on the east side of Manhattan. The most difficult problem Bush had to deal with was China. The United States had long opposed the right of Communist China, officially called the People's Republic of China, to take its seat at the United Nations. A rep-

At the United Nations. As permanent representative to the U.N., George Bush gained valuable experience in foreign policy.

resentative from Taiwan, which called itself the Republic of China, occupied China's seat. But since 1949, the government of Taiwan's Republic of China controlled little more than the island of Taiwan and a few tiny islands nearby.

The U.S. Congress was split on the China question. Some senators and representatives accepted the People's Republic of China as a reality and suggested that the United States accept the transfer of the UN seat from Taiwan to China. Others vowed never to abandon Taiwan's leader Chiang Kai-shek, who had been an ally of the United States during World War II. President Nixon finally decided on a policy of dual representation. The United States would recognize the People's Republic of China at the UN but would also recognize Taiwan as the legitimate government of China.

This policy, called the One-China policy, allowed the United States to claim they recognized Communist China as a legitimate nation while also claiming that the United States had not abandoned Chiang Kai-shek as the ruler of China. This confusing policy was really just an elaborate game allowing all three parties to say that their interests were being justly represented. •

In July 1971, President Nixon announced that he would visit the People's Republic of China. Bush was as surprised as the rest of the nation by the sudden change in policy. "At this moment I don't know what our China policy in the UN will turn out to be," he wrote in his diary, "but all the UN people feel that the ball game is over. Peking [the capital of mainland China] is in and Taiwan is out."

As the question of who would occupy the Chinese seat at the UN neared a vote, Bush campaigned for the American position that both mainland China and Taiwan should have a voice in the UN. "I want you and the others in Congress to know," Bush wrote to one senator, "we are leaving no stone unturned here in our effort to win the issue. I have talked personally to some sixty-five representatives of foreign nations."

However, the international community had slowly accepted the reality of a Communist China; Britain and France had already opened diplomatic relations with China. Ultimately, the U.S. position lost out. The People's Republic of China took Taiwan's seat at the UN, and Taiwan was expelled. "I felt it was a dark moment for the United Nations and international diplomacy," wrote Bush.

Watergate

Bush had little time to stew over the defeat because a scandal was unfolding in Washington. In the early morning hours of June 17, 1972, five burglars were caught breaking into the Watergate complex in Washington, D.C. They had been ransacking the files of the Democratic national headquarters. The press jumped on the story, asking who was behind the burglary.

Details of a wider conspiracy emerged as the story unfolded. In January 1973, President Nixon recalled Bush from the United Nations and asked him to take over as chairman of the Republican National Committee. At the time, the press was tracking the Watergate burglary closer and closer to the Republicans. "I spent an enormous amount of time as chairman," Bush wrote, "trying to reassure [Republican members] that our political system was sound, that the Republican National Committee, thus the party, had nothing to do with Watergate, and that our president was innocent."

In late April 1973, the Watergate scandal had been tracked to Nixon's top aides. Bush was outraged. "I share your indignation," he wrote to a reporter. "Putting it on a very personal basis, everything that my father stood for in life seems from time to time threatened by the arrogant behavior of a handful of people."

Bush believed that, with the dismissal of Nixon's top aides, the scandal was over. But President Nixon approved the creation of a special prosecutor's office to investigate the Watergate break-in. Over the following months, more and more evidence indicated that Nixon had known about the burglars' plans. Nixon became hostile to Special Prosecutor Archibald Cox, and national opinion swung against the president. Nixon had become a pathetic figure, suspected and accused by the press.

"I was deeply offended and amazed," Bush wrote about Nixon's possible involvement. On August 7, 1974, Bush wrote a letter to President Nixon. "It is my considered judgment," he wrote, "that you should now resign. I expect in your lonely embattled position this would seem to you as an act of disloyalty from one you have supported and helped in so many ways." On August 9, Nixon resigned as president of the United States, and his vice president, Gerald Ford, was sworn in as president. "The day was unreal," Bush wrote in his diary. "A pall was over the White House."

Special Envoy to China

President Ford inherited a presidency racked by scandal. He determined to make a fresh start, trying to regain confidence in the Republican Party and the office of the presidency. He rewarded Bush for serving as the Republican national chairman in such a difficult time by letting him choose his next assignment. "After much thought, and after discussing it with Barbara," Bush wrote, "I decided what I really wanted to do was represent the United States in China."

Nixon had opened relations to China with his visit to Beijing. But much work was left to be done to reach normal relations. Bush spent the next fourteen months as head of the U.S. Liaison Office in Beijing. He and Barbara studied Chinese and learned as much as they could about China's culture. "Life here is really different," he wrote home to his children, "a world of contrast. The society is closed, no dissent, no real freedoms; and yet they've made much progress from the bad old days with people dying on the street."

China was most sensitive about being pushed around by what they called "American imperialists." Bush's main function was to set a tone of friendliness and respect. This was Bush's strength, and he won the trust and friendship of many Chinese government officials while discussing difficult steps in opening relations. Bush's informality was a hallmark of his days in Beijing. "I am wearing my PLA [Chinese People's Liberation Army] hat, my Marlbor-

Traveling in Peking. President Ford appointed Bush as special envoy to the People's Republic of China.

ough-country wool jacket, sometimes my Chinese overcoat," he wrote. "The diplomats look askance at this informality, or at least some do."

Into the Shadows

Because Bush did such a good job in China, President Ford recalled him from Beijing and offered him an even more sensitive position—director of the Central Intelligence Agency (CIA). At the time, the CIA was in trouble. Bush's role, once again, would be that of a troubleshooter. He had to revamp the agency, raise the morale of its agents, and win back the trust of the American people.

Bush looked at his new assignment with some reservations. "It's a graveyard for politics," he wrote to his siblings, "and it is perhaps the toughest job in government right now." Bush aired some of the CIA's dirty laundry in public and set out to restructure the agency, replacing top personnel and reining in covert operations. He also fought to keep a substantial budget for the spy organization because he felt that it was crucial to American foreign policy to have reliable, timely intelligence about international threats.

Bush liked the world of secret intelligence gathering, and slowly won the respect of the CIA staff.

But President Ford lost the election of 1976 to Democrat Jimmy Carter. Carter replaced Bush with a new man, and Bush's career as a diplomat and Republican troubleshooter came to an abrupt end. He packed his bags and moved back to Texas.

WHITE HOUSE, ACT ONE

WHEN BUSH RETURNED to private life, he accepted the chairmanship of Houston's First National Bank. After all this time, he found himself in his father's old business. The bank job gave Bush some time to sort through his options, and he worked at the bank only a day or so a week.

Through his years of government service, Bush had accumulated a vast network of powerful friends and supporters. He decided to draw on his support in May 1979, announcing his bid for the presidency of the United States. First, he had to win his party's nomination, thereby ensuring the full support of the national Republican Party.

Announcing his candidacy. In 1979, Bush decided to run for the presidency of the United States.

His opponent for the Republican nomination was an affable former actor from California named Ronald Reagan. Reagan had a knack for making Americans proud to be American and proved unusually popular among blue-collar workers, farmers, and Southerners, who were traditional Democrats.

Reagan campaigned on a conservative platform. He vowed to raise the budget for the military, reduce the role of the federal government, balance the budget, and cut taxes. Bush presented a more moderate Republican voice and called Reagan's economic plan "voodoo economics." Bush could simply see no way that Reagan's budget plan could work.

Though Bush made a strong showing early on, it soon became clear that Reagan had captured the mood of the country. His tough American talk reminded people of the greatness of the American republic, a message that soothed the ache of difficult financial times under Jimmy Carter.

Reagan won the Republican nomination and chose George Bush as his running mate. Bush was able to help Reagan with foreign policy. The phrase "voodoo economics," however, came back to haunt Bush when, as the vice-presidential candidate, he had to endorse Reagan's economic plan.

President Ford (right) supported running mates Ronald Reagan (center) and George Bush at the 1980 Republican National Convention.

Reagan and Bush won a stunning victory in the 1980 election and were sworn into office the following January. Aside from the ability to cast a tie-breaking vote in the Senate, the vice president is limited to what the president allows him to do. Fortunately for Bush, Reagan liked to delegate responsibility. Bush attended Reagan's national security briefings and was soon appointed chairman of the National Security Council crisis-management team. Bush's experience at the CIA and in foreign policy gave him a good grasp on some of the difficult security questions he had to address. In particular, he made plans to combat drug smuggling, terrorism, and crime.

Two months into Bush's term as vice president, a lone gunman shot and seriously wounded President Reagan. Although Reagan recovered quickly, the event underscored the vice president's primary role—second in command to the president. The U.S. Constitution lays out the succession clearly: If the president dies in office, the vice president serves out the rest of his term.

Bush was an ambassador for Reagan's foreign policy. He shuttled around the world meeting with foreign leaders to explain the policies of the United States. This was a tough job at the height of the Cold War between the United States and the Soviet Union. Reagan could be a somewhat flustered speaker on some subjects, but nothing moved him to eloquence as much as his hatred of the Soviet government, which he referred to as the "evil empire."

This approach frightened Americans and world leaders alike. They wondered if the man in the White House was the reckless cowboy that he had once played in films. Bush had the difficult task of explaining Reagan's open hostility toward the Soviets to leaders around the globe.

In 1984, Reagan and Bush ran for a second term. Bush worked tirelessly for reelection. Bush and Reagan were reelected, sweeping forty-nine states.

The Iran-Contra Affair

During Reagan's second term, Bush continued with his work on antiterrorism. "The U.S. government will make no concessions to terrorists," he said. "It will not pay ransoms, release prisoners, change its policies, or agree to other acts which might encourage additional terrorism."

But then a complicated international arms deal came to light during Reagan's second term. One of Reagan's national security council staff, Robert (Bud) McFarlane, raised the possibility of trading American weapons to Iran for the release of seven American hostages held prisoner in Lebanon. The hostages included William Buckley, the CIA station chief for Lebanon. Reagan feared that Buckley could be tortured into giving his captors sensitive information about U.S. military and intelligence operations.

The swap eventually took place. Arms were traded for hostages. Then some of the money gained from the arms sale was funneled to rebels fighting the government of Nicaragua. U.S. support for the rebels, called the Contras, was a typical Cold War operation. When the story finally broke that arms had been traded to Iran for the release of American hostages and that some of the money from the exchange had been given to the Contras, President Reagan came under intense criticism. It was suspected that Reagan and Bush had hatched the shady deal together.

Bush admitted that he had known about the sale of arms to Iran, but said he did not know they were part of a hostage deal. Bush also denied knowing anything about money being sent to the Contras. The press continued to criticize them, however, and Bush continued to defend himself and the president. "There's a lot at stake here," he wrote, "some of it relates to the president's very ability to govern for two years." It was later proven that Bush's aides met with representatives of the Contras, and many wondered how he could not have known about the deal. The Iran-Contra affair was one of Bush's greatest political problems—it left some voters doubtful about him.

The Fight of His Life

As early as 1984, during Reagan's reelection campaign, Bush had expressed a growing dissatisfaction with the vice presidency. "I get sick of vice presidential jokes," Bush wrote. He wanted to run on his own. "I'm beginning to think a little in my heart of hearts of the presidency," he wrote.

Bush's great obstacle was living up to Reagan's legacy. Reagan seemed strong and sure. He was the most popular and successful Republican president since Eisenhower. The subservient and usually toothless nature of the vice presidency, however, has always made it a difficult jumping-off point for a presidential campaign. Not since Martin Van Buren in 1836 had a vice president run successfully for the presidency.

Bush announced his candidacy in October 1987. A band played "The Yellow Rose of Texas," and he gave a speech calling for a "kinder, gentler nation," one that would look out for the needs of minorities and the forgotten man. He said he would accomplish this through "steady and experienced leadership," not through what he considered the failed social programs of the Democrats. "I am not a mystic," he said, "and I do not yearn to lead a crusade."

This message was too moderate for many of his conservative supporters. Just who was George Bush? People wondered whether he really was a Texan because he spent so much time in Kennebunkport, Maine. The carpetbagger accusation of twenty years earlier again reached his ears. *Newsweek* magazine ran a cover story on Bush with the title "Fighting the Wimp Factor." "The *Newsweek* story was the cheapest shot I've seen in my political life," he wrote in his diary. His advisors encouraged him to respond by picking a fight and showing that he could throw punches, too. "The 'wimp' cover," he wrote, "and then everybody reacts—pick a fight—be tough—stand for something controversial, etc., etc. Maybe they're right, but this is a hell of a time in life to start being something I'm not."

But Bush, who had gained a reputation at the White House as Mr. Polite, struck back with a surprisingly negative campaign against his Democratic rival, Michael Dukakis.

Dukakis was the governor of Massachusetts, one of the most staunchly Democratic states in the country. The two candidates were very different. Bush was an upper-class Yankee from an affluent family; Dukakis portrayed himself as a common man. Bush, standing 6 feet 2 inches (188 cm), towered over his rival when they appeared on the same stage for debates.

Shaking hands with 1988 Democratic presidential candidate, Michael Dukakis. Bush won forty-two states to defeat Dukakis in the election.

During the campaign, Dukakis boasted of the recent boom in the Massachusetts economy, which he called the "Massachusetts miracle," and pledged to do the same for the rest of the country if elected president. The U.S. economy was sluggish at that time, and Dukakis tried to peg Bush as a leader who cared more about foreign policy and military spending than about the economic welfare of Americans.

Bush responded by raising fears that Dukakis would cut military spending and raise taxes. In a speech he would later regret, Bush claimed firmly that he would not raise taxes. "Read my lips," he said, "no new taxes." Bush also characterized Dukakis as a "liberal outside the American mainstream," and accused him of being weak on crime.

The Republicans ran television ads about a man named Willie Horton. Willie Horton had been convicted of brutally killing a teenage gas-station attendant in Massachusetts. He was sentenced to life in prison. While Dukakis was governor, Horton had been set free for a weekend. Horton struck again. He kidnapped a young man and his fiancée in Oxon Hill, Maryland, beating both of them and raping the woman. The Republican ads depicted a revolving door with inmates passing into—and then immediately out of—a prison, while a somber voice said that Dukakis gave furloughs to "first-degree murderers not eligible for parole," and that some of them "committed other crimes like kidnapping and rape."

Dukakis defended the furlough program, which allowed prisoners to go free on weekends, arguing that it was designed to help prisoners back into normal life. The media picked up the story and publicized the Horton case even more. Rehabilitation of prisoners was unpopular with many voters, who preferred a president who would be tougher on crime and criminals.

Alhough the negativity of his campaign surprised many voters, Bush won forty-two states in the general election. At age sixty-four, Bush had been elected to the highest office in the United States. "Thank heavens it's over!" he wrote to Michael Dukakis.

WHITE HOUSE, ACT TWO

GEORGE BUSH WAS inaugurated on January 20, 1989. The next day, he and Barbara greeted tourists at the White House. The Bush White House was informal. If Bush did not have Reagan's regal nature and Hollywood appeal, he had an honest, reassuring manner. Unlike Reagan, Bush was a master of the process of government. The details of things interested him. He would not, like Reagan, delegate much of his presidential authority to subordinates. "George Bush is not only going to be the president," said a White House spokesman, "but he is also going to be very different from Ronald Reagan—familiar with the details,

On January 20, 1989, Barbara Bush looked on as her husband was sworn in as the forty-first president of the United States.

profoundly engaged with a lot of issues, right in the thick of it all."

Bush's first great challenge was to reduce the federal budget deficit. Under Reagan, the federal government spent more than it brought in through taxes. By the time Bush took office, the deficit had reached $170 billion. By 1988, Bush's old criticism of Ronald Reagan's national economic plan, the "voodoo economics" phrase that he had used in the 1980 election, had been borne out. The country had trouble repaying its loans and lacked funding for federal programs. Bush was determined to work with Democrats in Congress to reduce the deficit.

The Reagans were welcome visitors of President and Mrs. Bush at the White House.

To raise money for the federal budget, Bush raised taxes. He paid dearly for abandoning his "no new taxes" promise. His popularity fell.

Bush's great ability to compromise proved to be an asset, because Democrats controlled Congress. The president compromised on a federal budget package to avoid a government shutdown. He had to give up his demand to reduce the capital-gains tax.

Republican criticism of President Bush continued throughout his administration, but Bush concentrated on getting things done and passing bills with the support of Congress.

Bush passed some important legislation, such as the Americans with Disabilities Act. This act gave people with disabilities greater protections under the law. A revision of the Clean Air Act drastically increased environmental protections.

During his inauguration speech, Bush had called for a "kinder, gentler America," and he governed with a much friendlier style than the ideologically driven Reagan. Even his wife, Barbara, presented the image of a kindly, dignified first lady. Her white hair and her knack for humility and plain speaking gave her a natural charm that many Americans found endearing.

Signing the Americans with Disabilities Act. Bush's skill at compromise resulted in the passing of many bills into law.

George and Barbara's constant companion in the White House was their springer spaniel, Millie. Barbara Bush was never a high-profile first lady. She used her influence on George only in private. In 1990, Barbara Bush published a memoir, *Millie's Book*, written from the point of view of the First Dog. The brown-and-white canine briefly became a celebrity,

With the "First Dog." Millie proved not only to be a loyal companion but also a best-selling "author."

and the book raised more than $1 million for the Barbara Bush Foundation for Family Literacy.

Millie's Book also gave the First Dog a chance to respond to some negative publicity. The July 1989 issue of the *Washingtonian* called Millie the "Ugliest Dog." Bush found the incident amusing and protested to the editors of the *Washingtonian*. They apologized and sent Millie some dog biscuits. "Easy for the president to accept the apology," Millie wrote. "I did not."

Commander in Chief

In late December 1989, Panama, a small country at the narrowest part of Central America, had vital importance to the United States. It was the site of the Panama Canal. The canal allows U.S. commercial and military ships to sail from the Atlantic to the Pacific without going around South America. The Canal Zone was protected by the United States to avoid any possibility of closing the canal.

The leader of Panama was the corrupt Manuel Noriega. Bush was familiar with Noriega from his days as vice president. He knew that Noriega helped sell cocaine, most of which was headed for the United States. When Panamanians elected

Guillermo Endara, Noriega nullified the election. Television reports showed Noriega's thugs, called the Dignity Battalions, beating the vice-presidential candidate in the streets of Panama City.

One of Noriega's old friends, Major Moises Giroldi Vega, decided to try to take over Panama and asked the United States for help. Bush consulted with his national security advisors, who warned the president that they weren't sure what Giroldi was up to, or if he could be trusted to turn over Noriega to U.S. authorities who wanted to prosecute him on drug-trafficking charges. Bush waited. "Here it is 6 P.M.," he said, "and we don't know where Noriega is; we don't know whether he is wounded or not; and we don't know whether he is dead or alive." The coup attempt failed, and Giroldi and his rebels were executed by Noriega.

When news broke in the United States, Bush was criticized again. "I am not going to order kids into combat," Bush said in his defense, "without having reasonable intelligence assessments and without knowing what's going on."

While lawlessness in Panama continued, Bush looked for a way to arrest Noriega. He met with his advisors and planned an invasion. "All of us vowed never to let another such opportunity pass by," wrote Secretary of State James Baker. When Bush heard that an American officer and his wife had been tortured at the Comandancia, Noriega's headquarters, he was outraged. "I guess the thing that troubles me most," Bush said, "is the humiliation of the lieutenant's wife." He ordered Operation Just Cause—the invasion of Panama.

In the darkness of night on December 20, 1989, U.S. Army Rangers and paratroopers from the Eighty-Second Airborne Division descended on Panama. U.S. planes bombed Noriega's defenses from above. Bush stayed awake most of the night. "Those nineteen-year-olds who will be dropped in at night," Bush recorded, "I am thinking about the brutality of Noriega and what he's apt to do." The fighting was over by the next morning. Twenty-four Americans were killed, and 323 were injured. Endara, the elected president, took power. But Noriega had slipped away. For a few days, he hid out in the home of a Catholic priest. The U.S. offered a $1-million reward, while Noriega tried to arrange asylum in Spain. When Spain rejected him, he surrendered. Bush finally had his man. Noriega was flown to

Manuel Noriega, former leader of Panama. Today, he is serving time in an American prison.

Miami, Florida, where he was convicted of drug trafficking. He is serving his sentence in an American prison.

The Panama invasion and the capture of General Noriega made Bush very popular. Although the United Nations condemned the invasion, the people of Panama gave thanks. Even his critics at home admired Bush's handling of the situation.

In May 1990, Soviet leader Mikhail Gorbachev (left) joined President Bush for a historic summit in Washington.

Bush had earned a reputation as a master of foreign policy. His years of experience as special liaison to China and director of the Central Intelligence Agency were bearing fruit. In May 1990, the Soviet leader Mikhail Gorbachev came to Washington to meet Bush.

The Soviet Union was changing. Gorbachev had weakened the power of the Soviet Communist Party and opened the Soviet Union to the outside world. Members of the Communist Party opposed Gorbachev, so he looked to the United States for support.

The president seized the opportunity to open arms-control talks with the Soviet leader. Over the next three years, he signed treaties with Gorbachev that reduced the number of American and Russian nuclear weapons. Americans asked themselves if the Cold War might finally be at an end.

By November 1991, Poland, Czechoslovakia, Hungary, and other former Soviet-controlled countries declared their independence. Even East Germany, which had been occupied by Soviet forces since the end of World War II, was allowed to "go its own way," as Gorbachev put it. By the end of 1991, the Soviet Union ceased to exist. Gorbachev called President Bush at the White House on December

25 to tell him "you may feel at ease as you celebrate your Christmas."

Bush oversaw the collapse of America's most feared enemy. But that meant that America had to worry about the smaller countries that threatened the oil supply. Americans became more afraid of state-sponsored terrorism and biological and chemical weapons. In 1990, Saddam Hussein, the leader of Iraq, sent his army to invade Kuwait.

Operation Desert Storm

Iraqi tanks dashed toward Kuwait City, the capital of Kuwait, while troop carriers lurched behind them. By nightfall on August 2, Saddam Hussein was claiming victory for the "Revolution of August 2," as he called the invasion. Hussein had taken over Kuwait. Hussein argued that he was simply reclaiming what was once Iraqi territory. From 1980 to 1988, Hussein had led his country through a ruinous war against neighboring Iran. After eight years of war, Iraq was very poor. By invading rich Kuwait, Hussein thought he could restart the Iraqi economy.

President Bush was alarmed by the military buildup on the Iraq-Kuwait border, but America's ambassador to Iraq—April Glaspie—had told Hussein that the United States had "no opinion on the Arab-Arab conflicts, like your border disagreement with Kuwait." Hussein gambled that the United States would not go to war. Upon hearing of the invasion, Bush declared, "It will not stand." The Iraqi invasion left Americans stranded in the Persian Gulf region and threatened America's oil supply. To Saddam Hussein's surprise, the United Nations also condemned the invasion and called for Iraqi troops to withdraw.

Kuwait was not close to the United States like Panama was, and Bush could not just send an army of U.S. soldiers to invade an Arab nation without angering friendly Arab countries like Saudi Arabia and Egypt. So Bush gathered thirty nations, including Arab ones, into a coalition, or a group of armies. This coalition, the largest allied force assembled since World War II, was Bush's great diplomatic victory. And in January 1991, President Bush asked Congress for "all necessary means" to eject the Iraqis from Kuwait. Congress overwhelmingly supported the president.

At exactly 7 P.M. on January 16, the coalition forces began bombing Baghdad, Iraq's capital. Like

The burning oil fields of Kuwait. President Bush led a coalition of nations to fight the Iraqi forces invading that country.

most Americans, President Bush watched the bombardment on CNN, a cable news network that had cameras in the fire zone. Over the next month, American television featured repeated demonstrations of new "smart bombs" that destroyed buildings with pinpoint accuracy. The United States also bombed troop emplacements which left thousands of Iraqi soldiers dead in their trenches.

On February 23, special assault troops landed on the shores of Kuwait with speedboats, and tanks and helicopters crossed the border from Saudi Arabia into Iraq. The advance was slowed only by the vast number of Iraqi prisoners. The Iraqi soldiers were not willing to die for Saddam Hussein.

After 100 hours of ground assault, Bush called off Operation Desert Storm. "It was over," Bush wrote. "Saddam's army—what was left of it—was fleeing up what became known as the Highway of Death—the road between Kuwait City and Basra, just over the border in Iraq."

After the Persian Gulf War, Bush received fierce criticism for not capturing or killing Hussein. But Bush knew that Americans did not want their soldiers to die and that the Arab allies did not want American troops occupying an Arab country.

Meeting the troops. Bush traveled to Saudi Arabia and spent time with Americans serving in the Persian Gulf War.

Bush hoped instead that the Iraqi people would throw Saddam Hussein out. "I was convinced, as were all of our Arab friends and allies, that Hussein would be overthrown," he wrote. "That did not and has still not happened. We underestimated his brutality and cruelty to his own people and the stranglehold he has on his country." To this day, the United States enforces an embargo on Iraq and patrols a "no-fly" zone over parts of the country, restricting Saddam Hussein's ability to move troops. The matter is still unresolved.

Private Citizen

Bush's leadership in the Persian Gulf War led him to new heights of popularity. His mastery of international affairs was praised, and many Americans thought he showed how the United States could be strong and fair.

As the election of 1992 neared, Bush returned to the campaign trail. At first he was the easy favorite, because of his victory in the Gulf War. But as the election neared, his challenger, Arkansas governor Bill Clinton, stirred fears about the American economy. Bush had served the United States well in foreign policy, but Clinton promised to rekindle the U.S. economy. On November 3, 1992, when votes were counted, George Bush was told he would return to private citizenship. Bill Clinton had won the election.

On January 20, 1993, George Bush packed up, said good-bye to his staff, and boarded a plane for

George and Barbara Bush (with Dan Quayle and his family) bid farewell to the White House after President Clinton's election in 1992.

Houston. "January 20th was, indeed, a very emotional day in our lives; but now we are back, just plain private citizens, staying out of the public limelight and doing exciting things. By way of example: Barbara is a good cook. I am a good dishwasher."

Bush returned to private business and occasionally attended ceremonial functions as a former president. His family, he says, provides much of his
pleasure in private life. In 1995, he celebrated his
fiftieth year of marriage to Barbara Bush, and the
Bush family continues to gather regularly at the
Kennebunkport seaside retreat.

Celebrating his seventy-fifth birthday. George Bush enjoyed the company of his whole family for the 1999 occasion.

Through his family, Bush has also received a second life in politics—as the unofficial advisor to his sons. George W. Bush was elected governor of Texas in 1995, and Jeb Bush was elected governor of Florida in 1998. George W. Bush also

A clean jump. At age seventy-two, Bush fulfilled his longtime goal of parachuting from a plane just for fun.

announced his candidacy for the presidency in the election of 2000.

With the leisure time he has in private life, Bush was able to fulfill one long-standing ambition. When he had bailed out of his Avenger torpedo bomber in 1944, the young pilot had struck his head on the tail fin. He had always wanted to jump in peacetime. On March 25, 1997, seventy-two-year-old George Bush leaped from a plane over the Arizona desert at Yuma. An aerial snapshot shows a smiling Bush clad in a white jumpsuit skydiving with members of the Golden Knights parachute team.

TIMELINE

1924   George Herbert Walker Bush born on June 12 in Milton, Massachusetts

1942   Graduates from Phillips Academy, Andover, Massachusetts; enlists in U.S. Navy during World War II

1943   Receives gold wings, becoming the youngest naval aviator

1944   Shot down on September 2 by the Japanese near the island of Chichi Jima in the Pacific

1945   Marries Barbara Pierce on January 6; leaves the U.S. Navy in September

1948   Graduates Phi Beta Kappa from Yale University with a bachelor's degree in economics; moves to Odessa, Texas, to work as an equipment clerk for Dresser Industries/IDECO

1951   With John Overbey, founds Bush-Overbey Oil Development Company in Midland, Texas

1954   Bush-Overbey partners with Zapata Petroleum

1959	Moves to Houston, Texas, to run spin-off company, Zapata Off-Shore
1964	Runs for U.S. Senate but is defeated by Democratic incumbent, Ralph Yarborough
1967–71	Serves in U.S. House of Representatives
1971–73	Serves as U.S. ambassador to the United Nations
1973	Serves as chairman of the Republican National Committee
1974–75	Serves as U.S. special envoy to the People's Republic of China
1976–77	Serves as director of Central Intelligence Agency
1980	Is elected vice president of the United States as Ronald Reagan is elected president
1984	Reelected vice president on Reagan-Bush ticket
1988	Elected forty-first president of the United States
1992	Loses presidential election to William Jefferson Clinton
1993	Returns to private life in Houston, Texas
1997	George Bush Presidential Library at Texas A&M University is dedicated on November 6
1999	Son George W. Bush announces his bid for the 2000 presidential election

HOW TO BECOME A BUSINESS MANAGER

The Job

All types of businesses have managers, including food, clothing, banking, education, health-care, and business services. Managers make policies and carry out the firm's operations. Some managers supervise an entire company, or a geographical territory of a company's operations, such as a state. Other managers oversee a specific department, such as sales and marketing.

Business managers make sure the daily activities of a company or a department follow the company's overall plan. They set the organization's policies and goals. They may develop sales materials, analyze the department's budget, and hire, train, and supervise workers. Business managers often do the long-range planning for their company or department. This includes setting goals for the company and developing a plan for meeting those goals. A manager who is in charge of a single department might be asked to cooperate with other departments. A manager in charge of an entire company or organization usually works with the managers of various departments and oversees all departments.

If the business is privately owned, the owner may also be the manager. A large company, however, has a group of executives above the business manager.

Top executives, such as the company president, set the organization's goals and procedures. The chief executive officer, chief financial officer, chief information officer, executive vice presidents, and the board of directors assist them. Top executives plan future business goals and develop ways in which divisions and departments can work together to meet the company's goals. Sales and budgets are reviewed on a regular basis to check progress. The president also directs programs within the organization and sets aside the necessary funds. Dealing with the public is a big part of an executive's job. The president must deal with executives and leaders from other countries or organizations, and with customers, employees, and various special-interest groups.

Some companies have an executive vice president, who directs the activities of one or more departments, depending on the size of the company. In very large organizations, executive vice presidents may be highly specialized. For example, they may oversee the activities of business managers of marketing, sales promotion, purchasing, finance, personnel training, industrial relations, administrative services, data processing, property management, transportation, or legal services. In smaller organizations, an executive vice president might be responsible for several departments. Executive vice presidents also assist the president in setting and carrying out company policies and developing long-range goals. Executive vice presidents may serve as members of management committees on special projects.

Companies may also have a chief financial officer or CFO. In a small business, the CFO is usually responsible for managing money. This includes budgeting, capital expenditure planning, and cash flow, as well as financial reviews. In larger companies, the CFO may oversee financial-management departments. He or she will help help other managers develop financial and economic policies and carry them out.

Chief information officers, or CIOs, are in charge of their company's information technology. They determine how information technology can best be used to meet company goals. This may include researching, purchasing, and overseeing the set-up and use of technology systems, such as Intranet, Internet, and computer networks. These managers sometimes work on a company's Website, too.

Managers of companies that have several different locations may be assigned to specific geographic areas. For example, a large company with stores all across the United States is likely to have a manager in charge of each "territory." There might be a Midwest manager, a Southwest manager, a Southeast manager, a Northeast manager, and a Northwest manager.

Requirements

High School   The educational background of business managers varies widely. Many have a bachelor's degree in liberal arts or business administration. If you are interested in becoming a business manager, you should start preparing in high school by taking college-preparatory classes. Because the ability to communicate is important, take as many English classes as possible. Speech classes are another way to improve these skills. Courses in mathematics, business, and computer science are also excellent choices to help you prepare for this career.

Postsecondary   Business managers often have a college degree in a subject that meets the needs of the department they direct. For example, a degree in accounting for a business manager of finance; a degree in computer science for a business manager of data processing; and a degree in engineering or science for a director of research and development. As computer usage grows, managers are often expected to have experience with the information technology that applies to their field.

Many managers have graduate or professional degrees. Managers in highly technical manufacturing and research activities often have a technical or scientific master's degree or a doctorate. A law degree is necessary for managers of corporate legal departments, and hospital managers generally have a master's degree in health services administration or business administration.

Exploring

To get experience as a manager, start with your own interests. Managerial talents are used in any organized activity, whether you're involved in drama, sports, the school paper, or a part-time job. Managerial tasks include planning, scheduling, supervising other workers or volunteers, fund-raising, or budgeting. Local businesses also have job opportunities that give you firsthand knowledge and experience in management. If you can't get an actual job, try to set up a meeting with a business manager to talk with him or her about this career.

Employers

In 1998, the United States had more than 3.3 million jobs for general managers and executives, according to the U.S. Bureau of Labor Statistics. While these jobs were found in every industry, 60 percent of them were in the wholesale, retail, and service industries. In a 1998 survey of members of the American Management Association, 42.6 percent of the 4,585 participants worked in manufacturing. Approximately 32 percent worked in the services industry, which includes banking, health care, and the tourist industry.

Virtually every business in the United States hires managers. Obviously, the larger the company, the more such jobs it is likely to have. Companies doing business in larger geographical territories are likely to have more managers than those with smaller territories.

Starting Out

Generally, students interested in management need a college degree, although many retail stores, grocery stores, and restaurants hire promising applicants who have only a high-school diploma. Job seekers usually apply directly to the manager of such places. In some industries, management applicants need at least a bachelor's degree—either in a field related to the industry or in business administration. Often, they also need a graduate degree. A degree in computer science is an advantage. Your college placement office is often the best place to start looking for a job. Listings can also be found in newspaper help-wanted ads.

Many companies have management-trainee programs that college graduates can enter. Such programs are advertised at college career fairs or through college job-placement services. Often, however, management-trainee positions in business and government are filled by employees who already work for the organization and who show the traits needed for management.

Advancement

Lower-level employees who show managerial traits, such as leadership, self-confidence, creativity, motivation, decisiveness, and flexibility, fill most business-management and top-executive positions. In small firms, advancement to a higher management position may come more slowly than in larger firms.

Taking part in educational programs available for managers may speed up advancement. These are often paid for by the organization. Company training programs broaden knowledge of company policy and operations. Also consider training programs given by industry and trade associations and continuing-education courses in colleges and universities. These can inform managers of the latest developments in management techniques. In recent years, large numbers of middle managers were laid off when companies streamlined operations. As a result, competition for jobs is keen, and a commitment to improving your knowledge of the field and related subjects—especially computer information systems—may help set you apart.

Business managers may advance to executive or administrative vice president. Vice presidents may advance to top corporate positions—president or chief executive officer. Presidents and chief executive officers, upon retirement, may become members of the board of directors of one or more firms. Some business managers go on to establish their own companies.

Work Environment

Business managers usually have comfortable offices near the departments they direct. Top executives may have large offices and enjoy such privileges as executive dining rooms, company cars, country-club memberships, and liberal expense accounts.

Managers often travel between national, regional, and local offices. Top executives may travel to meet with leaders of other corporations, both within the United States and overseas. Meetings sponsored by industries and associations take place regularly and provide good opportunities to meet with peers and keep up with the latest developments. Large corporations often transfer people between the parent company and their other local offices or subsidiaries.

Earnings

Salary levels for business managers vary, depending upon the employee's level of responsibility and length of service, as well as the type, size, and location of the organization. Top-level managers in large firms earn much more than their counterparts in small firms. Also, salaries in large metropolitan areas such as New York City are higher than those in smaller cities and salaries in manufacturing and finance are higher than salaries in most state and local governments.

According to a 1998 survey by the American Management Association, the average base salary of U.S. managers was $92,700. Top executives of large corporations are the highest-paid management personnel. The average base salary for these managers is around $144,000. Lower-level managers might earn $55,000 to $60,000.

Benefits are usually excellent for business managers, and may even include bonuses, stocks, company-paid insurance premiums, company cars, country club memberships, expense accounts, and retirement benefits.

Outlook

Employment of business managers is expected to grow at about the same rate as other occupations through the year 2008, according to the U.S. Bureau of Labor Statistics. Many openings arise when managers are promoted, retire, or leave their positions to start their own businesses. The salary and prestige of these positions make them highly desirable, and competition will be intense.

Projected employment growth varies by industry. For example, employment opportunities in management in the computer and data-processing fields should double, while employment in manufacturing industries is expected to decline. Growth in service industries is expected to be faster than average.

TO LEARN MORE ABOUT BUSINESS MANAGERS

Books

Erlbach, Arlene. *The Kids' Business Book*. Minneapolis: Lerner, 1998.

Haskins, Jim. *African American Entrepreneurs*. New York: Wiley, 1998.

Nelson, Sharlene. *William Boeing: Builder of Planes*. Danbury, Conn.: Children's Press, 1999.

Older, Jules. *Anita!: The Woman behind the Body Shop*. Watertown, Mass.: Charlesbridge, 1998.

Websites

American Management Association

http://www.amanet.org

For news about management trends, resources on career information and finding a job, and an on-line job bank

Association for Women in Management
http://www.womens.org/
An organization that provides information about careers for women in management

Junior Achievement
http://www.ja.org
For information about programs for students in kindergarten through high school

Where to Write
American Management Association
1601 Broadway
New York, New York 10019-7420
212/586-8100

Association for Women in Management
927 15th Street, N.W., Suite 1000
Washington, DC 20005
202/216-0775

Junior Achievement
One Education Way
Colorado Springs, CO 80906
719/636-2474

National Management Association
2210 Arbor Boulevard
Dayton, OH 45439-1580
937/294-0421

HOW TO BECOME A GOVERNMENT OFFICIAL

The Job

Federal and state officials hold positions in the legislative, executive, and judicial branches of government at the state and national levels. They include governors, judges, senators, representatives, and the president and vice president of the country. Government officials are responsible for preserving the government against external and domestic threats. They also supervise and resolve conflicts between private and public interest, regulate the economy, protect the political and social rights of the citizens, and provide goods and services. Officials may, among other things, pass laws, set up social-service programs, and decide how to spend the taxpayers' money.

Think about the last time you cast a vote, whether in a school, local, state, or federal election. How did you make your decision? Was it based on the personal qualities of the candidate? The political positions of the candidate? Certain issues of importance to you? Or do you always vote for the same political party? As voters, we choose carefully when electing a government official, taking many things into consideration. Whether you're electing a new governor and lieutenant governor for the state, a president and vice president for the country, or senators and representatives for the state legislature or the U.S. Congress, you're choosing people to act on your behalf. The decisions of state and federal lawmakers affect your daily life and your future. State and federal officials pass laws that affect the arts, education, taxes, employment, health care, and other areas in efforts to change and improve communities and standards of living.

Nearly every state's governing body resembles that of the federal government. Just as the U.S. Congress is composed of the Senate and the House of Representatives, every state except Nebraska has a senate and a house. The president and vice president head the executive branch of the U.S. government, while the states elect governors and lieutenant governors. The governor is the chief executive officer of a state. In all states, a large group of officials handle agriculture, highway and motor-vehicle supervision, public safety and corrections, regulation of intrastate business and industry, and some aspects of education, public health, and welfare. The governor's job is to oversee their work. Some states also have a lieutenant governor, who serves as the presiding officer of the state's senate. Other elected officials commonly include a secretary of state, state treasurer, state auditor, attorney general, and superintendent of public instruction.

Besides the president and vice president of the United States, the executive branch of the national government consists of the president's cabinet. The cabinet includes the secretaries of state, treasury, defense, interior, agriculture, and health and human services. These officials are appointed by the president and approved by the Senate. The members of the Office of Management and Budget, the Council of Economic Advisors, and the National Security Council are also executive officers of the national government.

State senators and state representatives are elected to represent various districts and regions of cities and counties within the state. The number of members in a state's legislature varies from state to state. The U.S. Congress has 100 senators as established by the Constitution—2 senators from each state—and 435 representatives. (The number of representatives is based on a state's population—California has the highest number of representatives with 52.) The primary job of all legislators, on both the state and national levels, is to make laws. With a staff of assistants, senators and representatives learn as much as they can about the bills being considered. They research legislation, prepare reports, meet with constituents and interest groups, speak to the press, and discuss legislation on the floor of the House or Senate. Legislators also may be involved in selecting other members of the government, supervising the government administration, gathering and spending money, impeaching executive and judicial officials, and setting up election procedures, among other activities.

Requirements
High School Courses in government, civics, and history will help you gain an understanding of the structure of

state and federal governments. English courses are also important. You need good writing skills to communicate with your constituents and other government officials. Math and accounting will help you develop the analytical skills needed to understand statistics and demographics. Science courses will help you make decisions concerning health, medicine, and technological advances. Journalism classes will help you learn about the media and the role they play in politics.

Postsecondary State and federal legislators come from all walks of life. Some hold master's degrees and doctorates, while others have only a high-school education. Although most government officials hold law degrees, others have undergraduate or graduate degrees in such areas as journalism, economics, political science, history, and English. No matter what you majored in as an undergraduate, you'll likely be required to take classes in English literature, statistics, foreign language, Western civilization, and economics. Graduate students concentrate more on one area of study; some prospective government officials pursue a master's degree in public administration or international affairs. Take part in your college's internship program, which will involve you with local and state officials, or pursue your own internship opportunities. By contacting the offices of your state legislators and your state's members of Congress, you can apply for internships directly.

Other Requirements

Good "people skills" will help you make connections, gain election, and make things happen once you are in office.

You should also enjoy argument, debate, and opposition—you'll get a lot of it as you attempt to get laws passed. A calm temperament in such situations will earn the respect of your colleagues. Strong character and a good background will help you avoid the personal attacks that occasionally accompany government office.

Exploring

A person as young as sixteen years old can gain experience with legislature. The U.S. Congress, and possibly your own state legislature, has opportunities for teenagers to work as pages. They want young people who have demonstrated a commitment to government study. If you work for Congress, you'll be running messages across Capitol Hill, and you'll have the opportunity to see senators and representatives debating and discussing bills. The length of a page's service can be from one summer to one year. Contact your state's senator or representative for an application.

Become involved with local elections. Many candidates for local and state offices welcome young people to assist with campaigns. You'll make calls, post signs, and get to see a candidate at work. You'll also meet others with an interest in government, and your experience will help you gain a more prominent role in later campaigns.

Employers

State legislators work for the state government, and many hold other jobs as well. Because of the part-time nature of some legislative offices, state legislators may hold part-time jobs or own their own businesses. Federal officials work full-time for the Senate, the House, or the executive branch.

Starting Out

There is no direct career path for state and federal officials. Some stumble into their positions after some success with political activism on the grassroots level. Others work their way up from local government positions to state legislature and then into federal office. Those who serve in the U.S. Congress have worked in the military, journalism, academics, business, and many other fields.

Advancement

Initiative is one key to success in politics. Advancement can be rapid for someone who is a fast learner and is independently motivated, but a career in politics usually takes a long time to establish. Most state and federal officials start by pursuing training and work experience in their particular field, while getting involved in politics at the local level. Many people progress from local politics to state politics. It is not uncommon for a state legislator to eventually run for a seat in Congress. Appointees to the president's cabinet and presidential and vice presidential candidates have frequently held positions in Congress.

Work Environment

Most government officials work in a typical office setting. Some may work a regular 40-hour week, while others work long hours and weekends. One potential drawback to political life, particularly for the candidate running for office, is that there is no real off-duty time. The individual is continually under observation by the press and public, and the personal lives of candidates and officeholders are discussed frequently in the media.

Because these officials must be appointed or elected in order to keep their jobs, it is difficult to plan for long-range job objectives. There may be long periods of unemployment, when living off savings or working at other jobs may be necessary.

Frequent travel is involved in campaigning and in holding office. People with children may find this lifestyle demanding on their families.

Earnings

In general, salaries for government officials tend to be lower than salaries in the private sector. For state legislators, the pay can be very much lower. According to the NCSL, state legislators make $10,000 to $47,000 a year. A few states, however, don't pay state legislators anything but an expense allowance. And even those legislators who receive a salary may not receive any benefits. However, a state's top officials are paid better: The Book of the States lists salaries of state governors as ranging from $60,000 to $130,000.

The Congressional Research Service publishes the salaries and benefits of Congress members. Senators and representatives are paid $136,673 annually. Congress members are entitled to a cost-of-living increase every year but don't always accept it. Congressional leaders such as the Speaker of the House and the Senate majority leader receive higher salaries than other Congress members. For example, the Speaker of the House makes $171,500 a year and U.S. Congress members receive excellent insurance, vacation, and other benefits.

Outlook

To attract more candidates for legislative offices, states may consider salary increases and better benefits for state senators and representatives. But changes in pay and benefits for federal officials are unlikely. An increase in the number of representatives is possible as the U.S. population grows, but it would require additional office space and other costly expansions. For the most part, the structures of state and federal legislatures will remain unchanged, although the topic of limiting the number of terms a representative is allowed to serve often arises in election years.

The federal government has made efforts to shift costs to the states. If this trend continues, it could change the way state legislatures and executive officers operate in regards to public funding. Already, welfare reform has resulted in state governments looking for financial aid in handling welfare cases and job programs. Arts funding may also become the sole responsibility of the states as the National Endowment for the Arts loses support from Congress.

The government's commitment to developing a place on the Internet has made it easier to contact your state and federal representatives, learn about legislation, and organize a grassroots movement. This increase in voter awareness of candidates, public policy issues, and legislation may affect how future representatives make decisions. Also look for government programming to be part of cable television's expansion into digital broadcasting. New means of communication will involve voters even more in the actions of their representatives.

TO LEARN MORE ABOUT GOVERNMENT OFFICIALS

Books

Bonner, Mike. *How to Become an Elected Official.* Broomall, Penn.: Chelsea House, 2000.

Fish, Bruce, and Becky Durost Fish. *The History of the Democratic Party.* Broomall, Penn.: Chelsea House, 2000.

James. Lesley. *Women in Government: Politicians, Lawmakers, Law Enforcers.* Austin, Tex.: Raintree/Steck-Vaughn, 2000.

Lutz, Norma Jean. *The History of the Republican Party.* Broomall, Penn.: Chelsea House, 2000.

Websites

Congress.Org

http://www.congress.org/

A guide to Congress, providing information about House and Senate members as well as current bills and legislation

U.S. House of Representatives
http://www.house.gov
Provides a variety of information about the House of Representatives

U.S. Senate
http://www.senate.gov
Information about senators and how the Senate works

Where to Write
U.S. Senate
Office of Senator (Name)
United States Senate
Washington, DC 20515
202/224-3121

U.S. House of Representatives
Washington, DC 20515
202/224-3121

National Conference of State Legislatures
1560 Broadway, Suite 700
Denver, CO 80202
303/830-2200
For information about *State Legislatures Magazine*, and other information concerning state legislatures

TO LEARN MORE ABOUT GEORGE BUSH

Books

Greenberg, Judith E. *Barbara Pierce Bush*. Danbury, Conn.: Children's Press, 1999.

Heiss, Arleen McGrath. *Barbara Bush*. Broomall, Penn.: Chelsea House, 1992.

Kent, Zachary. *George Bush*. Chicago: Childrens Press, 1989.

Sandak, Cass R. *The Bushes*. New York: Crestwood House, 1991.

Websites

CIA Home Page
http://www.cia.gov/
The home page of the Central Intelligence Agency

George Bush
http://www.whitehouse.gov/WH/glimpse/presidents/html/gb41.html
A brief biography provided by the White House

George Bush Presidential Library
http://www.csdl.tamu.edu/bushlib/
The site for the George Bush Presidential Library at Texas
A & M University

The History Place
http://www.historyplace.com/speeches/bush-war.htm
The text of Bush's speech announcing Desert Storm

Interesting Places to Visit
The George Bush Presidential Library and Museum
1000 George Bush Drive
West College Station, Texas 77845
409/260-9552

United Nations
New York, New York 10017
212/963-4440

The U.S. Capitol
Washington, DC 20505
202/225-6827

The White House
1600 Pennsylvania Avenue, N.W.
Washington, DC 20502
202/456-7041

INDEX

Page numbers in *italics* indicate illustrations.

ABOUT THE AUTHOR

Robert Green holds an M.A. in Journalism from New York University and a B.A. in English literature from Boston University. He has written sixteen other books including a biography of John Glenn in the Ferguson Career Biographies and biographies of Alexander the Great, Tutankhamen, Julius Caesar, Hannibal, Herod the Great, and Cleopatra, as well as biographies of six British monarchs. He has also written a book on China for young adults and *"Vive La France": The French Resistance During World War II* and *Dictators of the Modern World*. He lives in New York City.